Contents

Slow Cooking Basics 2

Best-Loved Beef 4

Crowd-Pleasing Pork 22

Poultry in a Pot 40

Hearty Veggies & Sides 60

Savory Soups & Stews 78

Index 96

Slow Cooking Basics

This fast guide to slow cooking will enhance your experience and your results. You'll wonder how you ever got along without your Crock-Pot® slow cooker.

Stirring

Due to the nature of a slow cooker, there's no need to stir the food unless it specifically says to in your recipe. In fact, taking the lid off to stir food causes the slow cooker to lose a significant amount of heat, extending the cooking time required. Therefore, it's best not to remove the lid for stirring.

Cooking Temperatures and Food Safety

Cooking meats in your **CROCK-POT**® slow cooker is perfectly safe. According to the U.S. Department of Agriculture, bacteria in food are killed at a temperature of 165°F. Meats cooked in the **CROCK-POT**® slow cooker reach an internal temperature in excess of 170°F for beef and as high as 209°F for poultry. It's important to follow the recommended cooking times and to keep the cover on your **CROCK-POT**® slow cooker during the cooking process.

If your food isn't done after 8 hours when the recipe calls for 8 to 10 hours, this could be due to voltage variations, which are commonplace; to altitude; or even to extreme humidity. Slight fluctuations in power don't have a noticeable effect on most appliances; however, they can slightly alter the cooking times. Allow plenty of time, and remember:

It's practically impossible to overcook in a **CROCK-POT**® slow cooker. You'll learn through experience whether to decrease or increase cooking times.

Removable Stoneware

The removable stoneware in your **CROCK-POT**® slow cooker makes cleaning easy. Here are some tips on the use and care of your stoneware:

■ Don't preheat your **CROCK-POT**® slow cooker.

■ Your **CROCK-POT**® slow cooker makes a great server for dips, appetizers, or hot beverages. Keep it on the WARM setting to maintain the proper serving temperature.

■ Because all **CROCK-POT**® slow cookers have wrap-around heat, there is no direct heat from the bottom. For best results, always fill the stoneware at least half full to conform to recommended times. Small quantities can still be cooked, but cooking times will be affected.

Browning Meat

Meat cooked in the **CROCK-POT**® slow cooker will not brown as it would if it were cooked in a skillet or oven at high temperatures. For some recipes, it's not necessary to brown meat before slow cooking. If you prefer the flavor and look of browned meat, however, simply brown the meat in a large skillet coated with nonstick cooking spray before placing it in the stoneware and following the recipe as written.

Adding Ingredients at the End of the Cooking Time

Certain ingredients tend to break down during extended cooking. When possible, add these ingredients toward the end of the cooking time:

■ Milk, cream, and sour cream: Add during the last 15 minutes of cooking time.

■ Seafood: Add in the last 3 to 15 minutes, depending on the thickness and quantity. Gently stir periodically to ensure even cooking.

Cooking for Larger Quantity Yields

Follow these guidelines when preparing recipes in a larger unit, such as a 5-, 6-, or 7-quart **CROCK-POT**® slow cooker:

■ Roasted meats, chicken, and turkey quantities may be doubled or tripled, but seasonings should be adjusted by no more than half. Flavorful seasonings, such as garlic and chili powder, intensify during long, slow cooking. Add just 25 to 50 percent more spices, or as needed to balance flavors.

■ When preparing a soup or a stew, you may double all ingredients except seasonings (see above), dried herbs, liquids, and thickeners. Increase liquid volume by no more than half, or as needed. The **CROCK-POT**® slow cooker lid collects steam, which condenses to keep foods moist and to maintain liquid volume. Don't double thickeners, such as cornstarch, at the beginning. You may always add more thickener later, if needed.

■ When preparing dishes with beef or pork in a larger unit, such as a 5-, 6-, or 7-quart **CROCK-POT**® slow cooker, browning the meat in a skillet before adding it to the stoneware yields the best results; the meat will cook more evenly.

■ When preparing baked goods, it is best not to double or triple the recipe. Simply prepare the original recipe as many times as needed to serve more people.

Best-Loved Beef

Barley Beef Stroganoff

- ⅔ **cup uncooked pearl barley**
- 2½ **cups vegetable broth or water**
- 1 **package (6 ounces) sliced fresh mushrooms**
- ½ **teaspoon dried marjoram**
- ½ **pound 95% lean ground beef**
- ½ **cup chopped celery**
- ½ **cup minced green onion**
- ½ **teaspoon black pepper**
- ¼ **cup fat-free half-and-half**
  Minced fresh parsley (optional)

1. Place barley, broth, mushrooms and marjoram in **CROCK-POT®** slow cooker. Cover; cook on LOW 6 to 7 hours.

2. Cook and stir ground beef in large nonstick skillet over medium heat until browned and crumbly, about 7 minutes. Drain fat and discard. Add celery, green onion and pepper; cook and stir 3 minutes. Transfer to **CROCK-POT®** slow cooker.

3. Stir in half-and-half. Cover; cook on HIGH 10 to 15 minutes, until beef is hot and vegetables are tender. Garnish with parsley.

Makes 4 servings

Beef with Apples & Sweet Potatoes

Cut Sweet Potatoes

Beef Broth

1	boneless beef chuck shoulder roast (2 pounds)
1	can (40 ounces) sweet potatoes, drained
2	small onions, sliced
2	apples, cored and sliced
½	cup beef broth
2	cloves garlic, minced
1	teaspoon salt
1	teaspoon dried thyme, divided
¾	teaspoon black pepper, divided
1	tablespoon cornstarch
¼	teaspoon ground cinnamon
2	tablespoons cold water

1. Trim excess fat from beef and discard. Cut beef into 2-inch pieces. Place beef, sweet potatoes, onions, apples, broth, garlic, salt, ½ teaspoon thyme and ½ teaspoon pepper in **CROCK-POT**® slow cooker. Cover; cook on LOW 8 to 9 hours.

2. Transfer beef, sweet potatoes and apples to platter; cover with foil to keep warm. Let cooking liquid stand 5 minutes to allow fat to rise. Skim off fat and discard.

3. Stir together cornstarch, remaining ½ teaspoon thyme, remaining ¼ teaspoon pepper, cinnamon and water until smooth; stir into cooking liquid. Cook 15 minutes on HIGH or until cooking liquid is thickened. Serve sauce with beef, sweet potatoes and apples.

Makes 6 servings

Sloppy Sloppy Joes

4	**pounds ground beef**
1	**cup chopped onion**
1	**cup chopped green bell pepper**
1	**can (about 28 ounces) tomato sauce**
2	**cans (10¾ ounces each) condensed tomato soup, undiluted**
1	**cup packed brown sugar**
¼	**cup ketchup**
3	**tablespoons Worcestershire sauce**
1	**tablespoon dry mustard**
1	**tablespoon prepared mustard**
1½	**teaspoons chili powder**
1	**teaspoon garlic powder**
	Toasted hamburger buns

1. Brown beef 6 to 8 minutes in large skillet over medium-high heat, stirring to break up meat. Drain fat. Add onion and bell pepper; cook 5 to 10 minutes, stirring frequently, or until onion is translucent.

2. Transfer beef mixture to 4- to 5-quart **CROCK-POT®** slow cooker. Add remaining ingredients; stir until well blended.

3. Cover; cook on LOW 4 to 6 hours. Serve on buns.

Makes 20 to 25 servings

Best-Loved Beef

Hot Beef Sandwiches Au Jus

4 pounds beef rump roast
2 envelopes (1 ounce each) dried onion soup mix
2 teaspoons sugar
1 teaspoon dried oregano
1 tablespoon minced garlic
2 cans (10½ ounces each) beef broth
1 bottle (12 ounces) beer
  Crusty French rolls, sliced in half

1. Trim excess fat from beef and discard. Place beef in **CROCK-POT**® slow cooker.

2. Combine soup mix, sugar, oregano, garlic, broth and beer in large mixing bowl. Pour mixture over beef. Cover; cook on HIGH 6 to 8 hours or until beef is fork-tender.

3. Remove beef from **CROCK-POT**® slow cooker. Shred beef with two forks. Return beef to cooking liquid; mix well. Serve on crusty rolls with extra cooking liquid ("jus") on side for dipping.

Makes 8 to 10 servings

Slow-Cooked Pot Roast

1 tablespoon vegetable oil
1 beef brisket (3 to 4 pounds)
1 tablespoon garlic powder, divided
1 tablespoon salt, divided
1 tablespoon black pepper, divided
1 teaspoon paprika, divided
5 to 6 new potatoes, cut into quarters
4 to 5 medium onions, sliced
1 pound baby carrots
1 can (14½ ounces) beef broth

1. Heat oil on HIGH in **CROCK-POT®** slow cooker. Brown brisket on all sides. Transfer brisket to plate. Season with 1½ teaspoons garlic powder, 1½ teaspoons salt, 1½ teaspoons pepper and ½ teaspoon paprika; set aside.

2. Season potatoes with remaining 1½ teaspoons garlic powder, 1½ teaspoons salt, 1½ teaspoons pepper and ½ teaspoon paprika. Add potatoes and onions to **CROCK-POT®** slow cooker. Cook on HIGH, stirring occasionally, until browned.

3. Return brisket to **CROCK-POT®** slow cooker. Add carrots and broth. Cover; cook on HIGH 4 to 5 hours or on LOW 8 to 10 hours, or until beef is tender.

Makes 6 to 8 servings

Spicy Italian Beef

1 **boneless beef chuck roast (3 to 4 pounds)**
1 **jar (12 ounces) pepperoncini**
1 **can (14½ ounces) beef broth**
1 **bottle (12 ounces) beer**
1 **onion, minced**
2 **tablespoons dried Italian seasoning**
1 **loaf French bread, cut into thick slices**
10 **slices provolone cheese (optional)**

1. Trim fat from beef and discard. Cut beef, if necessary, to fit in **CROCK-POT®** slow cooker, leaving beef in as many large pieces as possible.

2. Drain pepperoncini; pull off stem ends and discard. Add pepperoncini, broth, beer, onion and herb blend to **CROCK-POT®** slow cooker; do not stir. Cover; cook on LOW 8 to 10 hours.

3. Remove beef from **CROCK-POT®** slow cooker; shred with two forks. Return shredded beef to cooking liquid; mix well. Serve on French bread, topped with cheese, if desired. Serve with additional sauce and pepperoncini, if desired.

Makes 8 to 10 servings

Tip: Pepperoncini are thin, 2- to 3-inch-long pickled mild peppers, available in the supermarket's Italian foods or pickled foods section.

Osso Bucco

1 large onion, cut into thin wedges
2 large carrots, sliced
4 cloves garlic, sliced
4 meaty veal shanks (3 to 4 pounds)
2 teaspoons herbes de Provence or
½ teaspoon each dried thyme,
rosemary, oregano and basil
1 teaspoon salt
½ teaspoon black pepper
¾ cup canned beef consommé or
beef broth
¼ cup dry vermouth (optional)
3 tablespoons flour
¼ cup minced parsley
1 small clove garlic, minced
1 teaspoon grated lemon peel

1. Coat **CROCK-POT®** slow cooker with nonstick cooking spray. Place onion, carrots and sliced garlic in bottom. Arrange veal shanks over vegetables, overlapping slightly, and sprinkle herbs, salt and pepper over all. Add consommé and vermouth, if desired. Cover; cook on LOW 8 to 9 hours or on HIGH 5 to 6 hours, or until shanks and vegetables are tender.

2. Transfer shanks and vegetables to serving platter; cover with foil to keep warm. Turn **CROCK-POT®** slow cooker to HIGH. Combine flour with 3 tablespoons water, mixing until smooth. Stir into cooking liquid. Cover; cook on HIGH 15 minutes or until sauce thickens.

3. Serve sauce over shanks and vegetables. Combine parsley, minced garlic and lemon peel; sprinkle over shanks and vegetables.

Makes 4 servings

BBQ Beef Sandwiches

1 **boneless beef chuck roast (about 3 pounds)**
¼ **cup ketchup**
2 **tablespoons brown sugar**
2 **tablespoons red wine vinegar**
1 **tablespoon Dijon mustard**
1 **tablespoon Worcestershire sauce**
1 **clove garlic, crushed**
¼ **teaspoon salt**
¼ **teaspoon liquid smoke**
⅛ **teaspoon black pepper**
10 **to 12 French rolls or sandwich buns, sliced in half**

1. Place beef in **CROCK-POT®** slow cooker. Combine remaining ingredients, except rolls, in medium bowl; pour over meat. Cover; cook on LOW 8 to 9 hours.

2. Remove beef from **CROCK-POT®** slow cooker; shred with two forks.

3. Combine beef with 1 cup sauce from **CROCK-POT®** slow cooker. Evenly distribute meat and sauce mixture among warmed rolls.

Makes 10 to 12 servings

Slow Cooker Brisket of Beef

1	whole well-trimmed beef brisket (about 5 pounds)
2	teaspoons minced garlic
½	teaspoon black pepper
2	large onions, cut into ¼-inch slices and separated into rings
1	bottle (12 ounces) chili sauce
12	ounces beef broth, dark ale or water
2	tablespoons Worcestershire sauce
1	tablespoon packed brown sugar

1. Place brisket, fat side down, in **CROCK-POT®** slow cooker. Spread garlic evenly over brisket; sprinkle with pepper. Arrange onions over brisket. Combine chili sauce, broth, Worcestershire sauce and sugar in medium bowl; pour over brisket and onions. Cover; cook on LOW 8 hours.

2. Turn brisket over; stir onions into sauce and spoon over brisket. Cover; cook on LOW 1 to 2 hours or until brisket is fork-tender. Transfer brisket to cutting board; cover with foil to keep warm. Let stand 10 minutes.

3. Stir cooking liquid, then let stand 5 minutes to allow fat to rise. Skim off fat and discard. (Cooking liquid may be thinned to desired consistency with water or thickened by simmering, uncovered, in saucepan.) Carve brisket across grain into thin slices. Spoon cooking liquid over brisket.

Makes 10 to 12 servings

Crowd-Pleasing Pork

Pork & Tomato Ragoût

2	pounds pork stew meat (1-inch cubes)
¼	cup all-purpose flour
3	tablespoons oil
1¼	cups white wine
2	pounds diced red potatoes
1	can (14½ ounces) diced tomatoes
1	cup finely chopped onion
1	cup water
½	cup finely chopped celery
2	cloves garlic, minced
½	teaspoon black pepper
1	cinnamon stick
3	tablespoons chopped fresh parsley

1. Toss pork with flour. Heat oil in large skillet over medium-high heat until hot. Add pork to skillet and brown on all sides. Transfer to **CROCK-POT®** slow cooker.

2. Add wine to skillet; bring to a boil, scraping up browned bits from bottom of skillet. Pour into **CROCK-POT®** slow cooker.

3. Add remaining ingredients except parsley. Cover; cook on LOW 6 to 8 hours, until pork and potatoes are tender. Discard cinnamon stick. Adjust seasonings. Top with parsley.

Makes 6 servings

Scalloped Potatoes & Ham

6 large russet potatoes, sliced into ¼-inch rounds

1 ham steak (about 1½ pounds), cut into cubes

1 can (10¾ ounces) condensed cream of mushroom soup, undiluted

1 soup can water

1 cup shredded Cheddar cheese

Grill seasoning, to taste

1. Layer potatoes and ham in **CROCK-POT®** slow cooker.

2. Combine soup, water, cheese and seasoning in large mixing bowl. Pour mixture over potatoes and ham.

3. Cover; cook on HIGH 3½ hours or until potatoes are fork-tender. Turn **CROCK-POT®** slow cooker to LOW and continue cooking 1 hour.

Makes 5 to 6 servings

Italian Sausage and Peppers

3 cups bell pepper chunks (1 inch), preferably a mix of red, yellow and green*

1 small onion, cut into thin wedges

3 cloves garlic, minced

4 links hot or mild Italian sausage (about 1 pound)

1 cup marinara or pasta sauce

¼ cup red wine or port

1 tablespoon cornstarch

1 tablespoon water

Hot cooked spaghetti

¼ cup shredded Parmesan or Romano cheese

Look for mixed bell pepper chunks at supermarket salad bars.

1. Coat **CROCK-POT**® slow cooker with nonstick cooking spray. Place bell peppers, onion and garlic in **CROCK-POT**® slow cooker. Arrange sausage over vegetables. Combine pasta sauce and wine; pour over sausage. Cover; cook on LOW 8 to 9 hours on HIGH 4 to 5 hours or until sausage is cooked through and vegetables are very tender.

2. Transfer sausage to serving platter; cover with foil to keep warm. Skim off and discard fat from cooking liquid.

3. Turn heat to HIGH. Mix cornstarch with water until smooth; add to **CROCK-POT**® slow cooker. Cook 15 minutes or until sauce has thickened, stirring once. Serve sauce over spaghetti and sausage; top with cheese.

Makes 4 servings

Pork Chops with Jalapeño-Pecan Corn Bread Stuffing

- **6 boneless loin pork chops, 1 inch thick (1½ pounds)**
- **¾ cup chopped onion**
- **¾ cup chopped celery**
- **½ cup coarsely chopped pecans**
- **½ medium jalapeño pepper, seeded and chopped**
- **1 teaspoon rubbed sage**
- **½ teaspoon dried rosemary**
- **⅛ teaspoon black pepper**
- **4 cups unseasoned cornbread stuffing mix**
- **1¼ cups reduced-sodium chicken broth**
- **1 egg, lightly beaten**

1. Trim excess fat from pork and discard. Coat large skillet with nonstick cooking spray; heat over medium heat until hot. Add pork; cook 10 minutes or until browned on both sides. Remove; set aside.

2. Add onion, celery, pecans, jalapeño pepper, sage, rosemary and black pepper to skillet. Cook 5 minutes or until onion and celery are tender.

3. Combine cornbread stuffing mix, vegetable mixture and broth in medium bowl. Stir in egg. Spoon stuffing mixture into **CROCK-POT®** slow cooker. Arrange pork on top. Cover; cook on LOW about 5 hours or until pork is tender.

Makes 6 servings

Note: For moister dressing, increase chicken broth to 1½ cups.

Slow Cooker Cassoulet

1 pound white beans, such as
   Great Northern

   Boiling water to cover beans

1 tablespoon butter

1 tablespoon canola oil

4 veal shanks, 1½ inches thick, tied
   for cooking

3 cups beef broth

4 ounces maple-smoked bacon or
   pancetta, diced

3 cloves garlic, smashed

1 sprig each thyme and savory
   (or a bouquet garni of 1
   tablespoon each)

2 whole cloves

   Salt and pepper, to taste

4 mild Italian sausages

1. Rinse and sort beans and place
in large bowl; cover completely with
water. Soak 6 to 8 hours or overnight.
(To quick-soak beans, place beans
in large saucepan; cover with water.
Bring to a boil over high heat. Boil
2 minutes. Remove from heat; let soak,
covered, 1 hour.) Drain beans; discard
water.

2. Heat butter and oil in large skillet
over medium-high heat until hot. Sear
shanks on all sides until browned.
Transfer to **CROCK-POT**® slow cooker.
Add broth, bacon, garlic, beans, herbs,
and cloves. Add enough water to
cover beans, if needed. Cover; cook
on LOW 8 hours. After about 4 hours,
check liquid and add boiling water as
needed.

3. Before serving, season with salt and
pepper. Grill sausages and serve with
cassoulet.

Makes 4 servings

Poultry in a Pot

Chicken with Italian Sausage

- **10 ounces bulk mild or hot Italian sausage**
- **6 boneless skinless chicken thighs**
- **1 can (about 15 ounces) white beans, rinsed and drained**
- **1 can (about 15 ounces) red beans, rinsed and drained**
- **1 cup chicken broth**
- **1 medium onion, chopped**
- **1 teaspoon black pepper**
- **½ teaspoon salt**
- **Chopped fresh parsley**

1. Brown sausage in large skillet over medium-high heat, stirring to break up meat. Drain fat and discard. Spoon sausage into **CROCK-POT®** slow cooker.

2. Trim fat from chicken and discard. Place chicken, beans, broth, onion, pepper and salt in **CROCK-POT®** slow cooker. Cover; cook on LOW 5 to 6 hours.

3. Adjust seasonings, if desired. Slice each chicken thigh on the diagonal. Serve with sausage and beans. Garnish with parsley.

Makes 6 servings

Old World Chicken and Vegetables

1 tablespoon dried oregano

1 teaspoon salt, divided

1 teaspoon paprika

½ teaspoon garlic powder

¼ teaspoon black pepper

2 medium green bell peppers, cut into thin strips

1 small yellow onion, thinly sliced

1 cut-up whole chicken (about 3 pounds)

⅓ cup ketchup

Hot cooked egg noodles

1. Combine oregano, ½ teaspoon salt, paprika, garlic powder and black pepper in small bowl; mix well.

2. Place bell peppers and onion in **CROCK-POT®** slow cooker. Add chicken thighs and legs and sprinkle with half of oregano mixture. Add chicken breasts and sprinkle on remaining oregano mixture. Cover; cook on LOW 8 hours or on HIGH 4 hours. Stir in ketchup and remaining ½ teaspoon salt.

3. Serve chicken and vegetables over noodles.

Makes 4 servings

Chicken Provençal

2 pounds boneless skinless chicken thighs, each cut into quarters

2 medium red peppers, cut into ¼-inch-thick slices

1 medium yellow pepper, cut into ¼-inch-thick slices

1 onion, thinly sliced

1 can (28 ounces) plum tomatoes, drained

3 cloves garlic, minced

¼ teaspoon salt

¼ teaspoon dried thyme

¼ teaspoon fennel seeds, crushed

3 strips orange peel

½ cup fresh basil, chopped

1. Place chicken, bell peppers, onion, tomatoes, garlic, salt, thyme, fennel seeds and orange peel in **CROCK-POT®** slow cooker. Mix thoroughly.

2. Cover; cook on LOW 7 to 9 hours or on HIGH 3 to 4 hours.

3. To serve, sprinkle with basil.

Makes 8 servings

Tip: For 5-, 6- or 7-quart **CROCK-POT®** slow cooker double all ingredients.

Easy Parmesan Chicken

- **8 ounces mushrooms, sliced**
- **1 medium onion, cut in thin wedges**
- **1 tablespoon olive oil**
- **4 boneless skinless chicken breasts**
- **1 jar (26 ounces) pasta sauce**
- **½ teaspoon dried basil**
- **¼ teaspoon dried oregano**
- **1 bay leaf**
- **½ cup (2 ounces) shredded part-skim mozzarella cheese**
- **¼ cup grated Parmesan cheese**
- **Hot cooked spaghetti**

1. Place mushrooms and onion in **CROCK-POT®** slow cooker.

2. Heat oil in large skillet over medium-high heat until hot. Lightly brown chicken on both sides. Place chicken in **CROCK-POT®** slow cooker. Pour pasta sauce over chicken; add basil, oregano and bay leaf. Cover; cook on LOW 6 to 7 hours or on HIGH 3 to 4 hours or until chicken is tender. Remove and discard bay leaf.

3. Sprinkle chicken with cheeses. Cook, uncovered, on LOW 15 to 30 minutes or until cheeses have melted. Serve over spaghetti.

Makes 4 servings

Fresh Herbed Turkey Breast

2	**tablespoons butter, softened**
¼	**cup fresh sage, minced**
¼	**cup fresh tarragon, minced**
1	**clove garlic, minced**
1	**teaspoon black pepper**
½	**teaspoon salt**
1	**split turkey breast (about 4 pounds)**
1½	**tablespoons cornstarch**

1. Combine butter, sage, tarragon, garlic, pepper and salt. Rub butter mixture all over turkey breast.

2. Place turkey breast in **CROCK-POT®** slow cooker. Cover; cook on LOW 8 to 10 hours or on HIGH 4 to 5 hours or until turkey is no longer pink in the center.

3. Transfer turkey breast to serving platter; cover with foil to keep warm. Turn **CROCK-POT®** slow cooker to HIGH; slowly whisk in cornstarch to thicken cooking liquid. When the sauce is thick and smooth, pour over turkey breast. Slice to serve.

Makes 8 servings

Tip: For 5-, 6- or 7-quart **CROCK-POT®** slow cooker, double all ingredients.

Mexican Chili Chicken

2	medium green bell peppers, cut into thin strips
1	large onion, quartered and thinly sliced
4	chicken thighs
4	chicken drumsticks
1	tablespoon chili powder
2	teaspoons dried oregano
1	jar (16 ounces) chipotle salsa
½	cup ketchup
2	teaspoons ground cumin
½	teaspoon salt
	Hot cooked noodles

1. Place bell peppers and onion in **CROCK-POT**® slow cooker; top with chicken. Sprinkle chili powder and oregano evenly over chicken. Add salsa. Cover and cook on LOW 7 to 8 hours or on HIGH 2 to 3 hours or until chicken is tender.

2. Transfer chicken to serving bowl; cover with foil to keep warm. Stir ketchup, cumin and salt into cooking liquid. Cook, uncovered, on HIGH 15 minutes or until hot.

3. Pour mixture over chicken. Serve chicken and sauce over noodles.

Tip: For thicker sauce, blend 1 tablespoon cornstarch and 2 tablespoons water. Stir into cooking liquid with ketchup, cumin and salt.

Makes 4 servings

Autumn Chicken

1 **can (14 ounces) whole artichoke hearts, drained**
1 **can (14 ounces) whole mushrooms, divided**
12 **boneless skinless chicken breasts**
1 **jar (6½ ounces) marinated artichoke hearts, with liquid**
¾ **cup white wine**
½ **cup balsamic vinaigrette**
  Hot cooked noodles
  Paprika for garnish (optional)

1. Spread whole artichokes over bottom of **CROCK-POT®** slow cooker. Top with half of mushrooms. Layer chicken over mushrooms. Add marinated artichoke hearts with liquid. Add remaining mushrooms. Pour in wine and vinaigrette.

2. Cover; cook on LOW 4 to 5 hours.

3. Serve chicken and sauce over noodles. Garnish with paprika, if desired.

Makes 10 to 12 servings

Thai Chicken

2½   **pounds chicken pieces**
1   **cup hot salsa**
¼   **cup peanut butter**
2   **tablespoons lime juice**
1   **tablespoon soy sauce**
1   **teaspoon minced fresh ginger**
    Hot cooked rice
½   **cup peanuts, chopped**
2   **tablespoons chopped fresh cilantro**

1. Place chicken in **CROCK-POT®** slow cooker. Combine salsa, peanut butter, lime juice, soy sauce and ginger; pour over chicken.

2. Cover; cook on LOW 8 to 9 hours or on HIGH 3 to 4 hours or until done.

3. Serve chicken and sauce over rice; sprinkle with peanuts and cilantro.

Makes 6 servings

Mu Shu Turkey

- **1** **can (16 ounces) plums, drained and pitted**
- **½** **cup orange juice**
- **¼** **cup finely chopped onion**
- **1** **tablespoon minced fresh ginger**
- **¼** **teaspoon ground cinnamon**
- **1** **pound boneless turkey breast, cut into thin strips**
- **6** **(7-inch) flour tortillas**
- **3** **cups coleslaw mix**

1. Place plums in blender or food processor. Cover; blend until almost smooth. Combine plums, orange juice, onion, ginger and cinnamon in **CROCK-POT**® slow cooker; mix well.

2. Place turkey over plum mixture. Cover; cook on LOW 3 to 4 hours.

3. Remove turkey from **CROCK-POT**® slow cooker. Divide evenly among tortillas. Spoon about 2 tablespoons plum sauce over turkey in each tortilla; top with about ½ cup coleslaw mix. Fold up bottom edge of tortilla over filling, fold in sides, and roll up to enclose filling. Repeat with remaining tortillas. Use remaining plum sauce for dipping.

Makes 6 servings

Easy Cheesy BBQ Chicken

6 boneless skinless chicken breasts (about 1½ pounds)
1 bottle (26 ounces) barbecue sauce
6 slices bacon
6 slices Swiss cheese

1. Place chicken in **CROCK-POT®** slow cooker. Cover with barbecue sauce. Cover; cook on LOW 8 to 9 hours. (If sauce becomes too thick during cooking, add a little water.)

2. Before serving, cut bacon slices in half. Cook bacon in microwave or on stove top, keeping bacon flat.

3. Place 2 pieces cooked bacon on each chicken breast in **CROCK-POT®** slow cooker. Top with cheese slices. Cover; cook on HIGH until cheese melts.

Makes 6 servings

Spinach Spoon Bread

1   **package (10 ounces) frozen chopped spinach, thawed and squeezed dry**
1   **red bell pepper, diced**
4   **eggs, lightly beaten**
1   **cup cottage cheese**
1   **package (5½ ounces) cornbread mix**
6   **green onions, sliced**
½   **cup (1 stick) butter, melted**
1¼   **teaspoons seasoned salt**

1. Coat **CROCK-POT®** slow cooker with nonstick cooking spray; preheat on HIGH.

2. Combine all ingredients in large bowl; mix well. Pour batter into prepared **CROCK-POT®** slow cooker. Cook, covered, with lid slightly ajar to allow excess moisture to escape, on LOW 3 to 4 hours or on HIGH 1¾ to 2 hours, or until edges are golden and knife inserted in center of bread comes out clean.

3. Loosen edges and bottom with knife and invert onto plate. Cut into wedges to serve. Or, serve bread spooned from **CROCK-POT®** slow cooker.

Makes 8 servings

Winter Squash and Apples

1 teaspoon salt
½ teaspoon black pepper
1 butternut squash (about 2 pounds), peeled and seeded
2 apples, cored and cut into slices
1 medium onion, quartered and sliced
1½ tablespoons butter

1. Combine salt and pepper in small bowl; set aside.

2. Cut squash into 2-inch pieces; place in **CROCK-POT**® slow cooker. Add apples and onion. Sprinkle with salt mixture; stir well. Cover; cook on LOW 6 to 7 hours or until vegetables are tender.

3. Just before serving, stir in butter and season to taste with additional salt and pepper.

Makes 4 to 6 servings

Spanish Paella-Style Rice

2   cans (14½ ounces each) chicken broth

1½   cups uncooked converted long-grain rice

1   small red bell pepper, diced

⅓   cup dry white wine or water

½   teaspoon saffron threads, crushed or ½ teaspoon ground turmeric

⅛   teaspoon red pepper flakes

½   cup frozen peas, thawed

     Salt, to taste

1. Combine broth, rice, bell pepper, wine, saffron and pepper flakes in **CROCK-POT®** slow cooker; mix well.

2. Cover; cook on LOW 4 hours or until liquid is absorbed.

3. Stir in peas. Cover; cook 15 to 30 minutes or until peas are hot. Season with salt.

Makes 6 servings

Southwestern Stuffed Peppers

4 green bell peppers

1 can (15 ounces) black beans, rinsed and drained

1 cup (4 ounces) shredded pepper-jack cheese

¾ cup medium salsa

½ cup frozen corn, thawed

½ cup chopped green onions with tops

⅓ cup uncooked long-grain white rice

1 teaspoon chili powder

½ teaspoon ground cumin

Sour cream (optional)

1. Cut thin slice off top of each bell pepper. Carefully remove seeds, leaving pepper whole.

2. Combine beans, cheese, salsa, corn, onions, rice, chili powder and cumin in medium bowl. Spoon filling evenly into each pepper. Place peppers in **CROCK-POT®** slow cooker.

3. Cover; cook on LOW 4 to 6 hours. Serve with sour cream, if desired.

Makes 4 servings

Hearty Veggies & Sides

Deluxe Potato Casserole

1 can (10¾ ounces) condensed cream of chicken soup

1 cup (8 ounces) sour cream

¼ cup chopped onion

¼ cup plus 3 tablespoons melted butter, divided

1 teaspoon salt

2 pounds red potatoes, peeled and chopped

2 cups (8 ounces) shredded Cheddar cheese

1½ to 2 cups stuffing mix

1. Combine soup, sour cream, onion, ¼ cup butter and salt in small bowl.

2. Combine potatoes and cheese in **CROCK-POT®** slow cooker. Pour soup mixture over potato mixture; mix well.

3. Sprinkle stuffing mix over potato mixture; drizzle with remaining 3 tablespoons butter. Cover; cook on LOW 8 to 10 hours or on HIGH 5 to 6 hours, or until potatoes are tender.

Makes 8 to 10 servings

Mama's Best Baked Beans

1 **bag (1 pound) dried Great Northern beans**
1 **package (1 pound) bacon**
5 **hot dogs, cut into ½-inch pieces**
1 **cup chopped onion**
1 **bottle (24 ounces) ketchup**
2 **cups packed dark brown sugar**

1. Soak and cook beans according to package directions. Drain and refrigerate until ready to use.

2. Cook bacon in large skillet over medium-high heat until crisp. Transfer to paper towels to drain. Cool, then crumble bacon; set aside. Discard all but 3 tablespoons bacon fat from skillet. Add hot dogs and onion. Cook and stir over medium heat until onion is tender.

3. Combine cooked beans, bacon, hot dog mixture, ketchup and brown sugar in **CROCK-POT**® slow cooker. Cover; cook on LOW 2 to 4 hours.

Makes 4 to 6 servings

Hearty Veggies & Sides

Cheesy Broccoli Casserole

- **2** packages (10 ounces each) chopped broccoli, thawed
- **1** can (10¾ ounces) condensed cream of celery soup
- **1¼** cups shredded sharp Cheddar cheese, divided
- **¼** cup minced onions
- **½** teaspoon celery seed
- **1** teaspoon paprika
- **1** teaspoon hot pepper sauce
- **1** cup crushed potato chips or saltine crackers

1. Coat **CROCK-POT®** slow cooker with nonstick cooking spray. Combine broccoli, soup, 1 cup cheese, onions, celery seed, paprika and hot sauce in **CROCK-POT®** slow cooker; mix well.

2. Cover; cook on LOW 5 to 6 hours or on HIGH 2½ to 3 hours, or until done.

3. Uncover; sprinkle top with potato chips and remaining ¼ cup cheese. Cook, uncovered, on LOW 30 to 60 minutes or on HIGH 15 to 30 minutes, or until cheese melts.

Makes 4 to 6 servings

Jim's Mexican-Style Spinach

3 packages (10 ounces each) frozen chopped spinach

1 tablespoon canola oil

1 onion, chopped

1 clove garlic, minced

2 Anaheim chilies, roasted,* peeled and minced

3 fresh tomatillos, roasted,** husks removed and chopped

6 tablespoons fat-free sour cream (optional)

To roast chilies, heat heavy frying pan over medium-high heat until drop of water sizzles. Cook chilies, turning occasionally with tongs, until blackened all over. Place chilies in brown paper bag for 2 to 5 minutes. Remove chilies from bag and scrape off charred skin. Cut off top with seed core. Cut lengthwise into halves. With a knife tip, scrape out veins and any remaining seeds.

**To roast fresh tomatillos, heat heavy frying pan over medium heat. Leaving papery husks on, cook tomatillos, turning often, until husks are brown and interior flesh is soft, about 10 minutes. When cool enough to handle, remove and discard husks.*

1. Place frozen spinach in **CROCK-POT**® slow cooker.

2. Heat oil in large skillet over medium heat until hot. Cook and stir onion and garlic until onion is soft but not browned, about 5 minutes. Add chilies and tomatillos; cook 3 to 4 minutes longer. Add mixture to **CROCK-POT**® slow cooker.

3. Cover; cook on LOW 4 to 6 hours. Stir before serving. Serve with dollops of sour cream, if desired.

Makes 6 servings

Skinny Corn Bread

1¼ **cups all-purpose flour**
¾ **cup yellow cornmeal**
¼ **cup sugar**
1 **teaspoon baking powder**
1 **teaspoon baking soda**
1 **teaspoon seasoned salt**
1 **cup fat-free buttermilk**
¼ **cup cholesterol-free egg substitute**
¼ **cup canola oil**

1. Coat **CROCK-POT®** slow cooker with nonstick cooking spray.

2. Sift together flour, cornmeal, sugar, baking powder, baking soda and seasoned salt in large bowl. Make well in center of dry mixture. Pour in buttermilk, egg substitute and oil. Mix in dry ingredients just until moistened. Pour mixture into **CROCK-POT®** slow cooker.

3. Cook, covered, with lid slightly ajar to allow excess moisture to escape, on LOW 3 to 4 hours or on HIGH 45 minutes to 1½ hours, or until edges are golden and knife inserted into center comes out clean. Remove stoneware from **CROCK-POT®** slow cooker. Cool on wire rack about 10 minutes; remove bread from stoneware and cool completely on rack.

Makes 8 servings

Tip: This recipe works best in round **CROCK-POT®** slow cookers.

Savory Soups & Stews

Spicy Cheese Soup

- **1 pound processed cheese, cubed**
- **1 pound ground beef, cooked and drained**
- **1 can (8¾ ounces) whole kernel corn, undrained**
- **1 can (15 ounces) kidney beans, undrained**
- **1 can (14½ ounces) diced tomatoes with green chilies, undrained**
- **1 can (14½ ounces) stewed tomatoes, undrained**
- **1 envelope taco seasoning**
- **1 jalapeño pepper, seeded and diced (optional)**
- **Corn chips (optional)**

1. Coat **CROCK-POT®** slow cooker with nonstick cooking spray. Add cheese, beef, corn, beans, tomatoes with chilies, tomatoes with juice, taco seasoning and jalapeño pepper, if desired. Mix well.

2. Cover; cook on LOW 4 to 5 hours or on HIGH 3 hours or until done.

3. Serve with corn chips, if desired.

Makes 6 to 8 servings

Parsnip and Carrot Soup

1 medium leek, thinly sliced
4 medium parsnips, peeled and diced
4 medium carrots, peeled and diced
4 cups fat-free chicken broth
1 bay leaf
½ teaspoon salt
½ teaspoon black pepper
½ cup small pasta, cooked and drained
1 cup low-fat croutons
1 tablespoon chopped Italian parsley

1. Coat small skillet with nonstick cooking spray. Heat over medium heat until hot. Add leek; cook and stir until golden. Transfer to **CROCK-POT**® slow cooker.

2. Add parsnips, carrots, broth, bay leaf, salt and pepper. Cover; cook on LOW 6 to 9 hours or on HIGH 2 to 4 hours, or until vegetables are tender.

3. Add pasta during last hour of cooking. Remove bay leaf before serving. To serve, sprinkle with croutons and parsley.

Makes 4 servings

Tip: For 5-, 6- or 7-quart **CROCK-POT**® slow cooker, double all ingredients.

Roast Tomato-Basil Soup

2 cans (28 ounces each) peeled whole tomatoes, drained and 3 cups liquid reserved

2½ tablespoons packed dark brown sugar

1 medium onion, finely chopped

3 cups chicken broth

3 tablespoons tomato paste

¼ teaspoon ground allspice

1 can (5 ounces) evaporated milk

¼ cup shredded fresh basil (about 10 large leaves)

Salt and black pepper, to taste

1. Preheat oven to 450°F. Line baking sheet with foil; spray with nonstick cooking spray. Arrange tomatoes on foil in single layer. Sprinkle with brown sugar and top with onion. Bake about 25 to 30 minutes or until tomatoes look dry and light brown. Let tomatoes cool slightly; finely chop.

2. Place tomato mixture, 3 cups reserved liquid from tomatoes, broth, tomato paste and allspice in **CROCK-POT®** slow cooker. Mix well. Cover; cook on LOW 8 hours or on HIGH 4 hours.

3. Add evaporated milk and basil; season with salt and pepper. Cook on HIGH 30 minutes or until hot.

Makes 6 servings

Simmering Hot & Sour Soup

2 cans (14½ ounces each) chicken broth

1 cup chopped cooked chicken or pork

4 ounces fresh shiitake mushroom caps, thinly sliced

½ cup sliced bamboo shoots, cut into thin strips

3 tablespoons rice wine vinegar

2 tablespoons soy sauce

1½ teaspoons chili paste or 1 teaspoon hot chili oil

4 ounces firm tofu, well drained and cut into ½-inch pieces

2 teaspoons sesame oil

2 tablespoons cornstarch

2 tablespoons cold water

Chopped cilantro or sliced green onions

1. Combine chicken broth, chicken, mushrooms, bamboo shoots, vinegar, soy sauce and chili paste in **CROCK-POT®** slow cooker. Cover; cook on LOW 3 to 4 hours or on HIGH 2 to 3 hours or until done.

2. Stir in tofu and sesame oil. Combine cornstarch with water; mix well. Add to soup and mix in well. Cover; cook on HIGH 10 minutes or until soup has thickened.

3. To serve, sprinkle with cilantro.

Makes 4 servings

Beef Stew with Bacon, Onion and Sweet Potatoes

- **1** pound beef for stew, cut into 1-inch chunks
- **1** can (14½ ounces) beef broth
- **2** medium sweet potatoes, peeled and cut into 2-inch chunks
- **1** large onion, cut into 1½-inch chunks
- **2** slices thick-cut bacon, diced
- **1** teaspoon dried thyme
- **1** teaspoon salt
- **¼** teaspoon black pepper
- **2** tablespoons cornstarch
- **2** tablespoons water

1. Coat **CROCK-POT**® slow cooker with nonstick cooking spray. Combine all ingredients, except cornstarch and water, in **CROCK-POT**® slow cooker; mix well. Cover; cook on LOW 7 to 8 hours or on HIGH 4 to 5 hours, or until meat and vegetables are tender.

2. With slotted spoon, transfer beef and vegetables to serving bowl; cover with foil to keep warm.

3. Turn **CROCK-POT**® slow cooker to HIGH. Combine cornstarch and water; stir until smooth. Stir into cooking liquid. Cover; cook 15 minutes or until thickened. To serve, spoon sauce over beef and vegetables.

Makes 4 servings

Beef Stew with Molasses and Raisins

- ⅓ cup all-purpose flour
- 2 teaspoons salt, divided
- 1½ teaspoons black pepper, divided
- 2 pounds beef for stew, cut into 1½-inch pieces
- 5 tablespoons oil, divided
- 2 medium onions, sliced
- 1 can (28 ounces) diced tomatoes, drained
- 1 cup beef broth
- 3 tablespoons molasses
- 2 tablespoons cider vinegar
- 4 cloves garlic, minced
- 2 teaspoons dried thyme
- 1 teaspoon celery salt
- 1 bay leaf
- 8 ounces baby carrots, cut in half lengthwise
- 2 parsnips, diced
- ½ cup golden raisins

1. Combine flour, 1½ teaspoons salt and 1 teaspoon pepper in large bowl. Toss meat in flour mixture. Heat 2 tablespoons oil in large skillet over medium-high heat. Add half of beef. Brown well; set aside. Repeat with remaining beef and 2 tablespoons oil.

2. Add remaining oil to skillet. Add onions. Cook and stir 5 minutes. Add tomatoes, broth, molasses, vinegar, garlic, thyme, celery salt, bay leaf and remaining ½ teaspoon salt and ½ teaspoon pepper. Bring to a boil. Add browned beef and boil 1 minute.

3. Transfer mixture to **CROCK-POT®** slow cooker. Cover; cook on LOW 5 hours or on HIGH 2½ hours. Add carrots, parsnips and raisins. Cook 1 to 2 hours longer or until vegetables are tender. Remove and discard bay leaf.

Makes 6 to 8 servings

Chicken and Black Bean Chili

> 1   **pound boneless skinless chicken thighs, cut into 1-inch chunks**
> 2   **teaspoons chili powder**
> 2   **teaspoons ground cumin**
> ¾   **teaspoon salt**
> 1   **green bell pepper, diced**
> 1   **small onion, chopped**
> 3   **cloves garlic, minced**
> 1   **can (14½ ounces) diced tomatoes, undrained**
> 1   **cup chunky salsa**
> 1   **can (16 ounces) black beans, rinsed and drained**
>   **Toppings: sour cream, diced ripe avocado, shredded Cheddar cheese, sliced green onions or chopped cilantro, crushed tortilla or corn chips**

1. Combine chicken, chili powder, cumin and salt in **CROCK-POT®** slow cooker, tossing to coat.

2. Add bell pepper, onion and garlic; mix well. Stir in tomatoes with juice and salsa. Cover; cook on LOW 5 to 6 hours or on HIGH 2½ to 3 hours, or until chicken is tender.

3. Turn **CROCK-POT®** slow cooker to HIGH; stir in beans. Cover; cook 5 to 10 minutes or until beans are heated through. Ladle into shallow bowls; serve with desired toppings.

Makes 4 servings

Beer and Cheese Soup

2 to 3 slices rye or pumpernickel bread
1 can (14½ ounces) chicken broth
1 cup beer
¼ cup finely chopped onion
2 cloves garlic, minced
¾ teaspoon dried thyme
6 ounces American cheese, shredded or diced
4 to 6 ounces sharp Cheddar cheese, shredded
1 cup milk
½ teaspoon paprika

1. Preheat oven to 425°F. Slice bread into ½-inch cubes; place on baking sheet. Bake 10 to 12 minutes or until crisp, stirring once; set croutons aside.

2. Combine broth, beer, onion, garlic and thyme in **CROCK-POT®** slow cooker. Cover; cook on LOW 4 hours.

3. Turn **CROCK-POT®** slow cooker to HIGH. Stir in cheeses, milk and paprika. Cover; cook 45 minutes to 1 hour or until soup is hot and cheeses are melted. Stir soup well to blend cheeses. Ladle soup into bowls; top with croutons.

Makes 4 servings

Tip: For 5-, 6- or 7-quart **CROCK-POT®** slow cooker, double all ingredients.

Great Chili

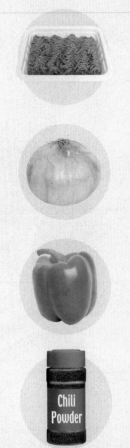

1½ pounds ground beef
1½ cups chopped onion
  1 cup chopped green bell pepper
  2 cloves garlic, minced
  3 cans (15 ounces each) dark red kidney beans, rinsed and drained
  2 cans (15 ounces each) tomato sauce
  1 can (14½ ounces) diced tomatoes, undrained
  2 to 3 teaspoons chili powder
  1 to 2 teaspoons dry hot mustard
  ¾ teaspoon dried basil
  ½ teaspoon black pepper
  1 to 2 dried hot chili peppers (optional)

1. Cook and stir ground beef, onion, bell pepper and garlic in large skillet until meat is browned and onion is tender. Drain fat and discard. Transfer mixture to 5-quart **CROCK-POT**® slow cooker.

2. Add beans, tomato sauce, tomatoes with juice, chili powder, mustard, basil, black pepper and chili peppers, if desired; mix well. Cover; cook on LOW 8 to 10 hours or on HIGH 4 to 5 hours.

3. If used, remove chili peppers before serving.

Makes 6 servings

Index

Autumn Chicken 52

Barbecued Pulled Pork
  Sandwiches 28

Barley Beef Stroganoff 4

BBQ Beef Sandwiches 18

Beef Stew with Bacon, Onion
  and Sweet Potatoes 86

Beef Stew with Molasses
  and Raisins 88

Beef with Apples & Sweet
  Potatoes. 6

Beer and Cheese Soup 92

Cheesy Broccoli
  Casserole. 72

Chicken and Black Bean
  Chili 90

Chicken Provençal 44

Chicken with Italian
  Sausage. 40

Deluxe Potato Casserole. . . 68

Easy Cheesy BBQ
  Chicken. 58

Easy Parmesan Chicken . . . 46

Fall-Off-the-Bone Ribs 36

Fresh Herbed Turkey
  Breast 48

Great Chili 94

Hot Beef Sandwiches
  Au Jus 10

Italian Sausage and
  Peppers 26

Jim's Mexican-Style
  Spinach. 74

Lemon Pork Chops 38

Mama's Best Baked
  Beans 70

Mexican Chili Chicken. . . . 50

Mu Shu Turkey 56

Old World Chicken and
  Vegetables. 42

Osso Bucco 16

Parsnip and Carrot Soup . . . 80

Pork & Tomato Ragoût 22

Pork Chops with Jalapeño-
  Pecan Corn Bread
  Stuffing 32

Pork Loin with Sherry
  and Red Onions 30

Roast Tomato-Basil Soup. . . 82

Scalloped Potatoes
  & Ham 24

Simmering Hot
  & Sour Soup 84

Skinny Corn Bread 76

Sloppy Sloppy Joes 8

Slow Cooker
  Brisket of Beef 20

Slow Cooker Cassoulet. . . . 34

Slow-Cooked Pot Roast. . . . 12

Southwestern Stuffed
  Peppers 66

Spanish Paella-Style Rice . . 64

Spicy Cheese Soup 78

Spicy Italian Beef 14

Spinach Spoon Bread 60

Thai Chicken 54

Winter Squash
  and Apples 62